THE COST OF THE RING

TWYLA D. HARRISON-NEALE

authorHOUSE®

AuthorHouse™
1663 Liberty Drive
Bloomington, IN 47403
www.authorhouse.com
Phone: 833-262-8899

Published by AuthorHouse 01/20/2022

ISBN: 978-1-6655-4423-8 (sc)
ISBN: 978-1-6655-4441-2 (e)

Print information available on the last page.

Any people depicted in stock imagery provided by Getty Images are models, and such images are being used for illustrative purposes only. Certain stock imagery © Getty Images.

This book is printed on acid-free paper.

Interior Image Credit: Baker Photography G'anecia Baker

*Gary Chapman Luke 14:28,29 KJV Proverbs 24:3 Hosea 1:1-3, 3:1
dictionary.com Philippians 4:11 dictionary.com 1 Corinthians 7:5-39 James
1:4 Ephesians 5:21-33 Genesis 3:20 Genesis 3:20 Lexicon H2332 Jeremiah
31:2-4 G2962 kyrios Ruth 2:1-13 Ecclesiastes 4:9-12 NLT Titus 2:3-5
Dictionary.com 1John 4:18 a strong feeling of wanting to have something or
wishing for something to happen. strongly wish for or want (something) 1
Corinthians 7:5 Jeremiah 31:3 Merriam-Webster.com Philippians 4:8 1 Peter
3:1 Proverbs 21:9 1 Corinthians 7:14 1 Peter 3:7 Ecclesiastes 3:1 Proverbs
25:24 Isaiah 26:3 (KJV) https://www.vocabulary.com/dictionary/peace*

*1 Corinthians 13:4-7, Merriam-Webster Genesis 2:16,
17 Proverbs 31 1 Corinthians 7:9 google.com*

*https://www.yourdictionary.com › Dictionary Definitions › lust
https://dictionary.cambridge.org/us/dictionary/english/lust
1 John 4:18 Ecclesiastes 3:1 Philippians 4:8-11
https://www.collinsdictionary.com/us/dictionary/
english/content Mark 10:9 1 Peter 3:7*

CONTENTS

DEDICATION

First and foremost I give glory, honor and praise to my Lord and Savior Jesus Christ! Without Christ I would be, and am nothing. Thank you for being a God of promises and most of all thank you for counting me as Your friend.

To my husband, Wayne Neale Jr., the man that stands by my side through every endeavor that I venture into by the leading of the Holy Spirit. You are my rock, my covering, my protector, my head and know that I love and appreciate you dearly. Thank you for trusting the Spirit of God on the inside of me. He blessed me with a jewel. I am proudly Mrs. Neale.

To my children: G'anecia Baker, D'quynton Thomas, Carlesia Hamm, Kyla Hamm (Wayne Neale III aka Tre'). You have walked with me through some dark places in life and that is a bond that will never be able to be taken from us. You all are a gift from God designed just for me and I love you with all of my heart.

To my late Apostle, Lathon Archie Jr., oh how I wish you were here to see this day, however; I find solace in knowing that you laid the foundation for me (and many others) to walk in. Rest well, you fought a good fight and there is a crown of righteousness awaiting you, sir. I will see you again

To my Apostle, Marnita Archie, you have been nothing less than a lady of grace, excellence and perseverance in all of the time that I have known you. Thank you for the push! Maturity is calling and we (the body) will answer. What if we unify? We will, we have!

To my circle of love that God has blessed me with who always encourages me to pursue destiny even in the face of pain, YOU ARE APPRECIATED!

FOREWORD

I applaud Minister Twyla Neale on this literary work that is of utmost importance to today's Christian society. The cost of the ring is a must read for all who may be contemplating marriage and it will serve as a textbook for those who have already entered into holy matrimony.

This extraordinary read is vital to the strengthening of today's generation- the generation that was born into a diluted dose of "holy matrimony"! It will ground on a solid foundation and equip you with the tools necessary for you to properly evaluate the cost.

For which of you, intending to build a tower, sitteth not down first, and counteth the cost, whether he have sufficient to finish it? Lest haply, after he hath laid the foundation, and is not able to finish it, all that behold it begin to mock him

As we move forward toward the culmination of this dispensation, the believer AND the world are almost identical in their posture on marriage and divorce! Is there a difference in the behavior of the Christian and the world? Faith and self-gratification? The rule of the Spirit of God and the rule of mankind?

This prayed out work, *The Cost of The Ring*, will reinforce the Bible teachings and ready the reader for bountiful benefits and blessings.

Sincerely rendered,
Apostle Marnita Archie

INTRODUCTION

For most little girls, their dream as a child is to grow up, get married, start a family and have children. It is forged in them as toddlers as we so lovingly call them "little momma" or when we buy them realistic baby dolls, toy strollers, or kitchen sets and watch as they pretend to play house.

Most definitely; the act of training our daughters to be great mothers and wives is an attribute that is greatly needed in the world we live in today. However; how often do we convey to our daughters that being whole, within themselves, single and successful and fulfilling the purposes of God is just as great of an achievement as being married? Do we as mothers and fathers reassure our daughters that being ALONE does not equate to being lonely?

The gift of singleness has its proper place in society just as marriage has its place. Somehow we have inadvertently conveyed the message that being married means you are whole and loved while being single means you are broken and undesirable which is obviously not factual.

While we encourage the nurturing behavior of our daughters we somewhat forget to forge this same nurturing quality into our sons. This is the beginning ingredient to a failed marriage. Toy strollers, baby dolls and dish sets give our daughters an idea of what marriage may entail but all the while we fail to give our sons this same preview as we discourage them from playing with dolls or even playing house by washing the pretend dishes.

Without realizing; we detour our sons from the idea of marriage, babies and anything attached to it as our daughters count down the hours until her big day.

Now, the issue with solely focusing on marriage and a white picket fence is that as we watch our girls develop over the course of their life we also see that the focus of this childhood dream shifts so often from marriage to the ring. We watch as our daughters put their candy rings on their ring finger, we listen as they confide in their friends about how they received a promise ring from their boyfriend and so on.

As our girls begin to enter into an adult relationship with the first sign that things between them and their significant other may be getting serious, many women begin to daydream about how big and beautiful her ring will be. They eagerly await the moment that they can announce to their friends and loved ones the day they will be united in matrimony with their mate. THEIR BIG DAY IS IN VIEW. They flash their engagement ring to every well-wisher they can find as if this "ring" represents the value of love that has been placed on them. Somehow we have allowed society to warp our thinking by equating the cost of our wedding ring to how much or less a man's love is for us. We see it in magazines, on TV and hear it in everyday talk how Mrs. X proudly showcases her 2 carat diamond. If a man doesn't provide a ring at all does that lessen his love? Of course not. If a man presents an elaborate ring does that mean his love is greater than the man that couldn't afford that kind of ring? Of course not.

A man proposes to his woman with a receipt of her $70k student loan debt being paid in full in place of a ring. She thanks him, but says she still requires a ring before getting married. What is she?

A. *Reasonable*
B. *Ungrateful*
C. *Smart*
D. *Dumb*

Social media source, Author unknown

The major problem with this train of thinking is that we have shifted our focus of what marriage truly is! It's not the amount of money spent on the wedding, it's not the number of people that show up to witness our vows, it's not how beautiful the venue is, it's not even how big or small your ring is. The focal point of every marriage is the covenant being made between the man, the woman and God.

The debate continues on whether the size of the ring matters or not and I will graciously step aside and let it continue. It's no secret that every woman loves to feel loved and loves receiving gifts from her husband or significant other but for just a few moments I would like to talk about *The cost of the ring* and not just the price of the ring. Some of you may be asking what the difference is, well I'm glad you asked! The price of the ring is merely how much was spent monetarily, but the cost of the ring is what both men and women pay mentally and physically in the marriage itself; maintaining a job when your mate doesn't have one! Standing by the side of an ill mate! Submitting your desires to your mates desires! Praying unselfishly for your mate even when you have come to a place of disagreement! This, my dear, is the real cost you pay for that dearly beloved ring. Later we will talk about how the husband and wife grow to become one flesh and in that chapter I pray that you will see that becoming one is an on-going process, a journey, and not a one-time event.

Throughout the years, a stigma has been placed on the idea of dating but the dating stage is one of, if not the, most important stages of a romantic relationship. At this stage you are able to completely be yourself with no pretenses. Remember to use wisdom but also be totally honest about what you want and what you are looking for. Believe me, there is someone that wants exactly what you want.

This stage is where you get to express your desires, likes, dislikes, fears, phobias, finances, sexual desires (or lack thereof) and deal breakers. Yes, let's talk about deal breakers! A deal breaker is something that you absolutely cannot live with or absolutely cannot live without. For example; if you are not a smoker, can't stand the smell of smoke, your eyes burn when you are around smoke and do not care to be in a relationship with a smoker, then smoking is definitely a deal breaker for you. If your deal breaker is lying and you cannot tolerate lying to any degree yet you find yourself dating someone that is constantly being caught in lies, then this relationship would need to end before a serious commitment took place. If you feel that you must have a companion that is affectionate and the person you are currently dating is not very touchy, doesn't like to hold hands, doesn't hug, is not a kisser then for you these qualities may cause you to reconsider the relationship because it's a deal breaker. If you are a clean freak but the person you are dating is the complete opposite of your definition of cleanliness then you may want to ask yourself if this is something you can live with because unless the Lord steps in, you will!

Basically, whatever you feel is an absolute must have or absolute cannot tolerate can be a deal breaker for you. What's important to note is that everyone's deal breakers will not be the same. What you may allow or accept another may not and each person must thoroughly evaluate this subject before entering into a serious lifetime commitment.

If you have reached a place in your relationship that marriage may be an option then I believe that all of the areas named need to be addressed. This is not the time to play shy or be coy. Be upfront and honest about your love language. If you ever get a chance to read the book *The 5 love languages* by Gary Chapman it is a wonderful tool for singles as well as married couples. Failure to address the subject of your love language can lead to major communication issues, unnecessary arguments and frustration in your marriage. If you have a high sex drive, say that! If you are a drinker, (socially or addicted) say that! If you are not a toucher, say that! The key is to be honest. Any other way of entering a relationship is considered manipulation, obtaining what you want based on a half-truth, basically and forthright, a lie.

Because divorce is at an all-time high, it is my sincere desire to help those that may be struggling in their marriage and even those that are preparing for marriage, to take a minute and evaluate the real cost of the ring before you say "I do" or even "I can't anymore". God created marriage and made it a beautiful institution IF both parties are willing to do what it takes to solidify the union. What must always be remembered is, MARRIAGE IS WORK.......! But the payout is great.

CHAPTER 1
THE COST

You are out on a date with the love of your life, you arrive at an expensive restaurant and as your mate ushers you out of the car, he gently embraces your hand with love and care. As you enter the restaurant you can't help but notice the ambiance of your surroundings as you arrive at your table. Thirty minutes into dinner, the waiter brings you the most beautiful dessert that you have ever seen. With the lights dim and candles burning, you cut into the dessert that was presented to you. On the inside you find your ring.....the ring you have dreamed about since you were a little girl. With tears in your eyes you hear those 4 words that will change your life forever "Will you marry me?" At that very moment nothing else is going through your mind except YES. The thought of bills, sickness, childbirth, unemployment, spiritual warfare, abuse (God forbid), infidelity, death etc. is the farthest thing from your mind. This is the place that most couples get stuck, but there is life beyond your yes.

To say "I do" means you are saying yes to every issue your mate may have. If it is low self-esteem, I do. If it is unemployment, I do. If it is illness or sickness, I do. You do not get to pick and choose what you will and will not commit or covenant too. Marriage is more than just wedding bells, babies and vacations. If I have said it once I'll say it again, marriage is work! What many people fail to ask themselves before committing to such a serious agreement is what the purpose of this union truly is. What will we gain from this union? And most importantly what has God said about this union?

As my Apostle encourages the married couples in our church, she reminds us that marriage should be a power move. You and your spouse should be able to build together, grow together and more importantly make up the deficits either one may have. Have you ever seen a couple and thought, he is so outgoing and she is so reserved? Or, she is so loud and he is so quiet? Although we chalk this up to opposites attract, this is exactly how a union should work. Where one partner is extreme, the other should bring calm. Where one partner may be laid back, the other should bring adventure. There should be a silent balance that causes that union to run like a well-oiled machine. Who has ever had a desert with only sugar in the recipe? Who has ever used a battery that only had a negative side? No one because it is going to take both the positive and negative, the bitter and the sweet issues in your marriage to create the masterpiece God has purposed for your union.

A house is built by wisdom and becomes strong through good sense.
By wisdom a house is built, and by understanding it is established;

Marriage, whether Godly or not, has the potential for success. Not every blooming, lasting marriage is God based and not every failed marriage is Godless. A house is built by wisdom and it becomes strong through good sense. Sex alone doesn't make a marriage. Loyalty alone doesn't make a marriage. Hold on for this next one, LOVE alone doesn't make a marriage! Of course these are attributes that you want and desire to be solid in a marriage but above all, and ultimately, wisdom according to the word, is what builds a home. What happens if one day you suffer an accident that prohibits you from satisfying your spouse sexually, is your marriage over? What do you do with the days that you don't feel like you love your spouse anymore, do you call it quits? What if infidelity is found in the marriage and the loyalty has been destroyed, is divorce inevitable? I venture to say no.

I am reminded of a story about a man who had a wife that repeatedly committed adultery, violating the covenant between the two. Not only did she commit adultery, she conceived children in her whoredom as well as birthing her lover a son. Regardless of how she strayed her husband would go and do whatever it took to bring her back to his side but she continued to find her way back to her adulterous lifestyle. How many men can say that they have experienced a love as devoted as this?

Do you recall the story of Jacob and Rachael? Jacob loved Rachael and asked her father to take her hand in marriage. The father agreed and told Jacob that he would have to work for him for seven years before he would give her to him. Because Jacob loved Rachael so much he agreed, worked his time and went on to say that seven years felt like days to him because he loved her so much. After the years were expired and Jacob was to receive his bride, he went in to know her (have sex with her) but when time came to consummate the marriage the older sister Leah had become his wife. Jacob was mortified. He asked the father "wasn't it Rachael that I worked for?" Of course it was but Jacob had been deceived and what was done could not be reversed.

Nevertheless; the father told Jacob, if you serve me for seven more years Rachael will be yours. Because of Jacob's love for Rachael he happily agreed and worked an additional seven years for her before she eventually became his wife. How many of you men can honestly say that if you saw a young lady, wanted a relationship with her, inquired about her through her father, asked for her hand in marriage and was told that you would have to work for him for seven years before you could take her as your own that you would do that? But wait, we're not done! The father tricks you and tells you a second time to work for him another seven years then you can take this young lady that you were so fond of in holy matrimony.

Have you found yourself in love to that degree or that committed to your potential wife? Jacob did and set a very high precedence for men today.

If you are saying you want a wife and you don't have a job, you are not ready to be married. Jacob worked 14 years to prepare for his wife. If you are saying that you want a wife and you have not shown undying love to her before you take her hand in marriage, you are not ready to be married. Jacob met every requirement set before him in order to take Rachael as his wife. You may have a desire to be married but are you willing to put in the work for your wife? Are you stable enough to meet the requirements for your wife?

Being ready (stable, healed and whole) and having a desire to get married are two very different things. Yes, God gave us the desire to have a companion but when our singleness has turned into a need to have a companion, there is a problem. The state of singleness should not be one of depression, frustration and feeling unfulfilled. To feel frustration in our state of singleness should be a sign that there is a void somewhere in our lives which means we are still fragmented, not whole. We are encouraged to be content in every state that we find ourselves in including the state of singleness. Content: in a state of peaceful happiness. A state of satisfaction.

Singleness is not a curse, and although sometimes we feel that it is, it is the state where we can live free of the responsibility of another. This is the time that we travel, see the world, save our finances and shed undesired baggage that could harm our future union. Foremost, the state of singleness should not be an idle state but time that we are able to devote ourselves totally to the work of the Lord and that is far greater than being devoted to any man or woman.

Ruth was a woman that was busy working and taking care of the widow when her future husband saw her from afar. He watched how she worked diligently in the field and how she catered to the widow until one day he inquired about her and ultimately married her. Ruth was not found in a state of depression because of her singleness. Ruth was not wallowing in loneliness but was busy living daily life. Because of her focus on the work that was before her, she became the owner of the very business she was so dedicated to. She was found in a state of contentment therefore; she qualified for promotion.

Once we have conquered the state of singleness we become eligible to move to another phase of our lives. The key is patience. The word of God tells us that when we let patience have its perfect work we will be perfect, entire, wanting nothing. Now, you are ready to be married.

As badly as we have represented the institution of marriage, the original design for our earthly marriage was to be a direct reflection of the spiritual marriage between Christ and His bride.

And out of your reverence for Christ be supportive of each other in love. For wives, this means being devoted to your husbands like you are tenderly devoted to our Lord, for the husband provides leadership for the wife, just as Christ provides leadership for his church, as the Savior and Reviver of the body. In the same way the church is devoted to Christ, let the wives be devoted to their husbands in everything.

And to the husbands, you are to demonstrate love for your wives with the same tender devotion that Christ demonstrated to us, His bride. For He died for us, sacrificing Himself to make us holy and pure, cleansing us through the showering of the pure water of the Word of God. All that He does in us is designed to make us a mature church for His pleasure, until we become a source of praise to Him—glorious and radiant, beautiful and holy, without fault or flaw.

Husbands have the obligation of loving and caring for their wives the same way they love and care for their own bodies, for to love your wife is to love your own self. No one abuses his own body, but pampers it—serving and satisfying its needs. That's exactly what Christ does for His church! He serves and satisfies us as members of His body.

For this reason a man is to leave his father and his mother and lovingly hold to his wife, since the two have become joined as one flesh. Marriage is the beautiful design of the Almighty, a great mystery of Christ and His church. So every married man should be gracious to his wife just as he is gracious to himself. And every wife should be tenderly devoted to her husband.

Let's back up just a little. The aforementioned quote says that husbands are to demonstrate love for their wives with the same tender devotion that Christ demonstrated to us, His bride...... All that He does in us, and for us, is designed to make us a mature church for His pleasure, UNTIL we become a source of praise to Him, UNTIL we be made glorious and radiant, UNTIL we become beautiful and holy, UNTIL we become without fault or flaw. He demonstrated love for us before we were what He wanted us to be. While we were yet sinners He showed the ultimate display of love and sacrificed Himself for us, the one He loves. He didn't wait until we got it together before He demonstrated His love for us, but He demonstrated it when we were at our worst. A huge problem in marriages today is that we try to wait for our spouse to be or do what we desire them to do before we release the love for them that should already be established. "When she acts right, then I'll......" "When he starts helping me with this housework then I'll......" that is what is called conditional or selfish love and should not be found in marriage.

Spouses, you cannot manipulate your mate by withholding love from them because they are not doing what you want them to do or may not be what you desire them to be anymore. On the contrary, men, you are to demonstrate love to her UNTIL she becomes the very reflection of what you are shaping her to be. Yes women, he is designed to shape you and that doesn't take away from your womanhood.

When man was created, God took the dust of the ground, formed it and blew the breath of life into him and named him Adam. When the woman was made God took a rib from the man, made the woman and presented her to her husband and her husband named her. God did not give Eve her name, her husband did. She became what he called her. If you are always calling her lazy, guess what, lazy is what you will have. If you are always calling her a bad wife, guess what, a bad wife is what you are going to have. If you are always calling her selfish, inconsiderate, one sided etc. then guess what, those attributes and qualities are what you will have. Eve became what her husband called her.

Did you ever notice that Adam did not name his wife until after they had experienced the greatest tragedy known to man-kind? In today's time we would equate their situation to that of irreconcilable differences. The woman had not only held an intimate conversation with a stranger but she literally obeyed the voice of someone other than her husband and caused calamity to come to their household. But even in the midst of tragedy and death Adam did not leave his wife but instead spoke life and hope to her, by calling her Eve, mother of the living. After God had declared death over them both, Adam declared life to his wife. As husbands you must love your wife until she becomes what you desire her to be just as our example did. With love and kindness one is drawn.

In the same manner, wives must submit to their own husband just as she submits to the Lord. Kind of hard to contemplate that whole submission thing, huh? Well, Sarah went so far as to call Abraham, her husband, lord. What she was in turn saying is, I submit to you as my head, covering and husband and likewise we are to follow suit. I hear some of you ladies now declaring "there is no way that I am calling Jim lord" and that may be true, the verbiage may not be the same but the reverence most definitely must be.

CHAPTER 2
DON'T JUST HEAR, LISTEN

One fundamental requirement to a strong relationship (of any kind) is communication. This can be verbal or non-verbal, facial expressions or body language. One key component to effective communication is knowing and understanding what communication type your partner understands. Some people do not respond to yelling and screaming therefore when they are approached with such communication, they shut down and subsequently nothing is received. Many people cannot stand to be ignored therefore when they are encountered with that type of behavior, they cannot function and subsequently nothing is received. Communication consists of more than merely uttering words to someone.

Communication means: *the act or process of using words, sounds, signs, or behaviors to express or exchange*

*information or to express your ideas, thoughts, feelings, etc.,
to someone else. : A message that is given to someone.*

The part I liked in this definition is *a message that is
given to someone*! If the person you are communicating
with has not received the message that you are trying to
give then there has been no effective communication.
What does that mean? Your partner may have heard what
you said but because of hardness, stonewalling, and pride
they did not fully receive your message. How will you
know if your spouse received your message or if they
just heard you? Ask them to repeat to you what you have
said, 9 times out of 10 it will not be the message you sent
but the message they interpreted through their guarded
perception. I have heard the jokes between men discussing
their wives and how we often ask "what did I say?" but that
is a great starting point to an open line of communication.

In addition; communication cannot and must not be
one sided. Let me explain. When you want to express your
feelings or maybe your point of view on a subject, you
desire understanding and attentiveness from the person
you are sharing it with. However; when the tables turn
you are defensive and close minded. That is not a healthy
relationship. One should not feel uneasy or guarded in any
healthy relationship but free and comfortable whether you
are agreeing or disagreeing. Communication should be
built firm and solid in the dating stage to avoid stumbling
blocks such as this in a marital setting. Remember, you
communicate by what is said as well as what is not said.
It is important to pay attention to both.

When we think or feel that love may be on the horizon we tend to get so engrossed with the idea of love that we ignore important signs, or unhealthy signs, of communication that a potential mate might display. The only thing we come to desire is for someone to love us, for someone to act like they care. Well in a lot of cases an act is all that it is. We often dismiss inappropriate behavior and comments with cute little phrases like "Girl, he works my nerves slamming these doors when he gets mad" or "This girl acts like a psycho when she doesn't get her way" "Girl, he is just saying that, he doesn't mean it". These actions and comments are displays of their true nature and feelings about you and do not need to be ignored. Love doesn't hurt! Love doesn't act unseemly! Love is patient! Love is kind! These aren't clichés; these are attributes that you should look for when you think you are in love or if someone tells you that they love you. In a nutshell, the very definition of what love is should be your measuring stick to gauge your relationship (of any nature).

As I have referenced, *The 5 love languages* is an amazing read for couples embarking on marriage. If you are not properly providing your spouse with the love that they need they may function in their marriage but will not flourish to the fullness of their ability.

A car that is designed to use a specific gas will operate at its full potential when you follow the guidelines set by the designer. Sure, you may spend your last penny to fill the tank with an alternative gas but again, it will not function at his optimum ability.

Once your spouse has expressed to you what it takes for them to operate at their maximum ability, listen and then fill their tank with what they need. If she has expressed to you her need for you to be present emotionally by spending time with her just to listen to her vent but you are focused on paying bills she is empty. If he has expressed to you his need to hear verbally that he is appreciated but you are consistent in keeping the house clean and a meal on the table, he is left empty.

These types of actions can leave both spouses feeling frustrated and unfulfilled. While you may be giving your all in the name of love and feel that it is being rejected, the reality is, it is not what is needed to satisfy the love gauge of your spouse. In loving someone it is important that you love them the way they need to be loved and not simply the way you want to love them. It is imperative that love is not thrown but given, not just accepted but received.

Every now and then it's ok to take inventory of your love tank. Love is patient, is your spouse patient with you? Love is kind, are you kind to your spouse? Love does not envy, do you find yourself in competition with your spouse? Love does not boast, do you make it awkwardly known when your idea was clearly the better idea? Love is not proud, do you purposely not apologize even when you aren't upset anymore? Love does not dishonor, do you put your spouse down in front of other people? Love is not self-seeking, do you put plans into place that will only benefit you? Love is not easily angered, are molehills that could easily be resolved made into mountains? Love keeps no record of wrongs, does your spouse always have to hear about the past 5 mistakes they made every time a disagreement comes up? Love does not delight in evil but rejoices with the truth, are you able to admit that your spouse was right even when it proves you wrong? Love always protects, does your spouse fear that you will not be there for them after an argument? Love always trusts, always hopes, always perseveres. **Love never fails!**

Take note of that very last statement, have you ever asked yourself what that statement truly means? Love never fails to be patient. Love never fails to be kind. Love never fails to display any of the characteristics listed above but rather will fulfill the responsibilities and duties of the covenant it entered into.

CHAPTER 3
THE DETACHMENT STAGE

*I*f you would allow me to use myself as an example, I was unmarried for 19 years before marrying my current husband. Sure I dated some here and there in that time but from marriage to marriage it was 19 years. In that time my children and I became very, very close. I had three daughters who became women and one son that developed into a man. As minors I was absolutely MOTHER but as the years matured I became FRIEND (that is possible). Once my husband came along and we knew that this was more than just a Friday evening bowling event or a Sunday night dinner date I had to come to the harsh reality that a certain level of separation had to take place between my children and myself. Where I would normally call my girls and tell them every aspect of my ups and downs I had to refrain! Up until this point, my girls knew everything about my life. My successes, my failures, my pain, my insecurities, my fears, everything BUT this was actually now my husband's position.

Not only did I have to make adjustments with my children, I had to make adjustments with my friends. Everything that took place in my relationship was not for public knowledge. This careless behavior gives the enemy (whoever/whatever your enemy is) an open invitation to take front row seating into your life. Of course, men and women alike should have healthy outside relationships with those they are able to share intimate moments with as well as sharing life events and experiences. However; it is important to evaluate who takes center stage in your life.

As a man one of your roles and instructions is to cover your wife not to strip her. When you share more of your feelings with others such as siblings, female friends, co-workers etc. verses with your wife you have allowed them to occupy the place that was meant for her to fill. Never, under any circumstance should you degrade your wife by exposing her flaws to anyone no matter how close your relationship to them is, this wreck-less talk will leave room for her to be stripped, uncovered and manipulated.

Part of covering your wife includes making your voice in the marriage louder than any voice from outside of your covenant. This has nothing to do with screaming and yelling but has everything to do with making your wife feel comfortable enough to submit to you in every area. The Lord God commanded Adam (the head) not to eat of the tree of the knowledge of good and evil but because he did not properly communicate with his wife there was room left open for the enemy to come in and clothe her with his thoughts, opinions and ideas. This improper covering brought death and destruction to their home and all of humanity.

Part of submitting to your husband includes consulting with him on new ideas especially if the idea is something that will affect your household. In the event that the idea is coming from a man then it most definitely must be submitted to the head of your home. It is not about whether the idea is good or bad but rather who it is you are allowing to cover you. How would you feel if you found out that your husband was taking his cue from Sally at work on how to run your home? I don't believe that would sit well with you just as it would not sit well with your husband to feel that Bob's voice was more influential than his.

Another phase of the detachment stage is closing yourself off from the outside chaos that may be taking place in the lives of your friends and acquaintances. Let me explain! If all you hear day in and day out is how your friend's wife is cheating on him or how your best girlfriend catches her husband in lie after lie or maybe how your friend found naked pictures and text messages to old boyfriends/girlfriends in their phone, eventually the perception of your spouse and marriage in general will begin to become extremely tainted. You will now begin to look for those traits and habits in your spouse. Even when they are not there your perception will tell you that they are. Basically; you will become paranoid and this will only cause chaos in your relationship. However; if we think on *whatever things are true, whatever things are honest, whatever things are just, whatever things are pure, whatever things are lovely, whatever things are of good report* we are promised peace.

Marriage is a sacred entity and a covenant between two people, YOU AND YOUR SPOUSE! Not your mother, not your father, not your siblings, not your children, not your friends and most definitely not mere acquaintances. To believe that constantly hearing about toxic relationships will not make you toxic is to believe that constantly drinking will not make you a drunk, constantly doing drugs will not make you an addict or constantly stealing will not make you a thief.

As a spouse, we must make every effort to surround ourselves with positive married couples that are of like minds striving to produce healthy, flourishing unions. We must work equally as hard to guard ourselves against the marriages and relationships that are bitter, angry and unwilling to put in the work for a successful union and ultimately hinder them from bringing forth the beautiful portrait God intended marriage to be.

When evaluating the detachments that need to take place in your life there are some things that can be considered. Whenever I was faced with going into a relationship I always tried not to go into it with a lot of do's and don'ts, likes and dislikes but I would tell my potential mate "if you don't want me to do it to you, then don't do it to me". In my eyes, this covered it all from talking on the phone with the opposite sex, riding in a vehicle with the opposite sex, to staying out until late night/early mornings. So how do you evaluate if a line has been crossed? How do you determine what is too much? When you know that the actions you are displaying would offend you if the tables were turned, then it's too much. In short; don't expect to get anything out of a relationship that you are not willing to put in. If this rule stays in its proper place then detachment and boundaries should come easy. At the first sign that boundaries have not been set, address it!

I don't care how long you have been friends with someone, if it violates the covenant that you have made with your spouse then correction is needed. Any true friend will respect your spouse and will desire for you to have the healthiest marriage possible and will make the decision, themselves, to take a step back if they detect turbulence.

Sometimes what may seem innocent to you may be huge to your spouse. Once you become married it is not mandatory that you disconnect from your single friends but you, and them, must understand that the relationship will most definitely be adjusted. You may not get to make every outing or every fishing trip. There may be times you really want to go but you must think about the state it will leave your family in! Will your husband be left to tend to all of the children alone after a long day of work? Did your wife have to finish the house work, cook, and help the kids with homework all on her own? These types of decisions can cause arguments that can easily be avoided with a simple "not tonight man" or "maybe next time sis".

The detachment stage includes more than just your personal circle, it includes ALL social media outlets as well. In the age we live in it is so easy to release our frustrations through social media and label it as "just keeping it 100" but there is just as much danger in this outlet as it is with your inner circle. When there are issues that need to be resolved in a relationship it needs to be addressed outside the confines of social media, friends and sometimes even family. It is not okay to spill out everything that you are feeling or everything that you may be going through at that particular moment on Facebook, Instagram, twitter or snap chat then hashtag it with "this applies to everyone" or "I'm just saying". You know how we do. The problem with this attempt to generalize these frustrations is that the person in which you are referring to (which is often your spouse) knows that these comments belong to them and this only adds to whatever issues are already brewing. Whether it is your spouse, sibling, relative or just a friend believe me they know these comments are theirs.

Social media is not the place to release your frustrations, especially the ones stemmed from within your marriage. You have to make a conscious effort to detach yourself from anything that is not pushing you closer to becoming one with your spouse. If there is an issue inside your marriage, your spouse should be the one, and only one, that you release everything too because it will ultimately be the two of you that commit or decide to quit the relationship.

Sometimes it is difficult to detach from a relationship that we have had for a significant amount of time so we justify the attachment with sayings like "but they always give me good advice" or "they encourage me to stay with him/her" or "they really wish me well". With all due respect their intentions and motives don't matter. The loyalty of that friendship has been fulfilled! It's not what the outsiders are saying, it's the position that they hold. The first person that should share in your happiness, sadness, hurts, pain, success, promotions, demotions, and life changes is your spouse. If the first person you seek advice from or share life events with is your girlfriend or your best bro, or in my situation my children, then that person holds a higher position with you than your spouse. But wives aren't you supposed to be his rib? His help meet? The closest thing to him? Husbands, shouldn't the void that you once felt now be filled by your wife?

In addition; spouses, when you fail to address this stage in marriage, you will find yourself jealous of the woman that means you no harm and does not want your husband or paranoid with every man that speaks to your wife. All that's needed are simple boundaries.

I read a powerful statement on a social site that said "*protect your marriage from the unmarried, never married, can't get married and couldn't stay married.*" This was one of the most profound statements that I had heard in a long time. No one can seek resolution for your marriage but you and your spouse. Do you protect your marriage the same way you protect your car? The same way you protect your jewelry? The same way you protect your collectibles? If not, what value have you placed on the union that you are expecting to yield you the greatest return?

CHAPTER 4
LANGUAGE

*W*omen, by nature, have the capability to produce a sharp tongue. However; in our frustration we forget that our words frame our world. We forget that life and death lie in the words that we speak. Divorcee's, never tell your current spouse that they are just like your ex! In their mind all they hear is failure. After all, the relationship that you have just referenced has failed. As much as it is possible try not to ever speak things out of anger. Never speak to your spouse in a derogatory manner or condescending tone. This is not only a reflection of how you are attempting to make them feel but it is also a reflection of you as their mate.

The word of God expresses clearly the importance of the words a wife speaks to her husband. She has the power to build him or destroy him simply by the words she speaks to him, about him, and over him. *It's better to live alone in the corner of an attic than with a quarrelsome wife in a lovely home.* Let's pause here for one moment. In the beginning when God created man He said it is not good for man to be alone therefore; He made woman for man, a suitable helpmeet. There was something so important that a woman possessed that God said man should not be without her. But Solomon states, exclaims rather, that it is better to live alone than to live with a quarreling woman! To me that is powerful. Because Solomon knew the impact that a woman's word carries, he felt it would be better to live alone than to be framed negatively by the words of a contentious woman. Did we forget that a sanctified wife can sanctify her household? Ladies, remember we talked about different forms of communication? You can win him with and through your behavior, actions and chaste conversation. Everything doesn't require a rebuttal and every conversation won't end at your last word.

When communicating with our spouse we must be aware of the tone in which we use and the energy that is already evident. If there is already negative energy present when wanting to address an unpleasant situation, the conversation can escalate and become damaging instead of bringing resolve. Both parties must remain open minded and sarcasm free. Ladies, oftentimes we do not realize that our know it all responses are still words spoken negatively and are still somewhat sarcastic. Even if you are right, it's not necessary that you prove it every time! What are "know it all responses" you might ask? Well, when your husband tells you "Randy is going to pick up the kids for soccer practice today" and you respond "yeah, I know, I talked to Sharon already". That is a know it all response. When your husband tells you "I figured out what that noise was in the kitchen, it was a screw making a funny noise on the washing machine" and you respond "I saw that earlier today". That is a know it all response. Sometimes the only response needed is "okay baby" or "thank you for fixing that". These types of responses are the kind of responses that can build your husband up and allow him to confidently feel like the head of his home instead of silently feeling that he is unneeded and unvalued in the marriage. It's also called submission. You do not have to prove that you already knew the information he provided (even if you did). The need to always convey that you were right can be portrayed as negative language and in all honesty, it is a form of pride.

Submission is something that is rejected at the very mention of the word. Somehow we have concluded that submission is a sign of weakness but that couldn't be farther from the truth. To submit yourself to a cause means that you exercise total control and demonstrate the ability to yield your strength to another strength. Every battle is not to be fought, peace is the goal.

More than just words

While we examine ourselves and the language that we use to communicate, we must realize that our language goes far beyond mere words. Our body actions, how we respond and relate to people, our facial expressions (RBF) and how we treat others can all be defined as language! When your mate tells you that they do or do not like a thing and you continue to do or not do what they have clearly conveyed bothers them, you have spoken loud and clear to them that you do not care about their feelings. When you can't have a decent conversation with your spouse without rolling your eyes, huffing and puffing, shaking your head (you know how it gets) trust me, that language is being heard louder than the words you may be speaking verbally.

What does it really say about us?

In every immature argument that takes place there are a lot of low blows that are thrown but if all of those things that you say about your spouse in the heat of the moment are true, what does it really say about you? Didn't you choose that mate? Didn't you say yes to the person that you now see as less than? Husbands have you forgotten that you are now her, wives have you forgotten that you are now him!

Once the dust settles and you reconcile, is your spouse still stupid? Is your spouse still ugly? Do you still hate her/him? Is your spouse still any of the things that you spewed out in your anger? Are the feelings for your spouse the same as what you spewed out in the heat of the moment? If your answer is yes then what does that say about you for becoming one with that type of person? If your answer is no then how do you rebound from such language and damaging behavior? Pride can be one of the biggest destroyers in marriage that causes this type of language to be ignored and not addressed but as hard and uncomfortable it may seem after the dispute, these comments and behavior must be addressed and not simply swept under the rug. Furthermore; it is imperative that this language is never used again.

Chapter 5
KNOW THE TRIGGERS

*I*n a later chapter we will discuss the process of becoming one with your spouse but for just a moment let's talk about the triggers that keep you separate. As you learn more and more about your mate's child-hood, their past relationships, their hurts, their vulnerabilities, addictions they may have had to overcome etc. you must also pay close attention to what their triggers are.

Triggers are words, situations, or places that spark a memory of hurt or simply a place in one's past that brings them discomfort. In marriage we cannot purposely use these triggers to get back at our mate or cause intentional pain. This information was given at a moment they felt the most connected to you. Never would they have divulged that type of information if they knew that there was a chance that they would have to revisit the place that brought them so much pain.

A trigger can be anything from seeing your mate wear an inappropriate outfit, watching certain movies, to leaving empty bottles around the house. Let me explain; when my husband and I got married he would leave empty bottles everywhere around the house. Alcohol bottles, peroxide bottles, juice bottles, shampoo bottles, milk bottles and any kind of bottle we had in the house. This would drive me up a wall until one day I asked "Babe, why do you leave all of these empty bottles around the house? If they are empty, throw them away" his reply was "when we were little, there were so many of us so we all may not have had a glass to drink from. We would have to fill up any kind of bottle we had and use them".

Even though I knew that he did not expect us to use these bottles for this purpose in our marriage, this broke my heart because this was a trigger for him. It took him back to an undesired place in his life. A couple once told me that they would be sitting at home having family time and watching movies when all of a sudden there would be an awkward silence in the room. In the movie, there was a scene where the wife was having an affair and the husband found out about it. Because this woman was in tune with her husband and had already communicated with him intimately about his past, she leaned over and asked "Is this hard for you to watch?" His reply was "yes" so the couple turned from that movie and chose to watch something else. This was a trigger that took him back to an undesired place in his life before his current marriage.

A woman that was recently married experienced a trigger in her relationship early on that had to be addressed quickly if her marriage was to have any chance of lasting. In her younger days she had been raped multiple times leaving her very defensive when it came to the opposite sex. Although she was healed from the experiences themselves, there were still triggers. When her husband wanted to be intimate with her he had to be careful in how he approached her. If he hugged her too tight, trigger! If he turned over in the middle of the night to caress her without her prior knowledge, trigger! He would tell her on many occasions how she jerked and pulled away from him through the night but because she was reacting from her subconscious, she would deny these accusations not realizing that it was in fact the truth. If the couple had not addressed this issue it would have been easy for the husband to internalize that and feel rejected by his wife. In fact; her trigger became a trigger for him! When the wife would pull away from him, it would trigger the spirit of rejection that he had fought so hard to renounce. Once the husband understood that this was merely a trigger for her and not an action directed towards him, they could move forward in finding a resolution in that area.

On one occasion, a husband and wife stopped by a family member's home, the wife went in and the husband waited in the car. A few minutes into his wait he felt that it would be okay to go around the corner to the store. When the wife came out to leave the husband had in fact gone around the corner to the store without telling her. When the wife came out and saw that the car and her husband were gone she immediately went into panic mode! This was a trigger of abandonment for her. As a child she was not raised by her mother but by her grandmother and she never knew her father. The root of rejection and abandonment was buried deep within her. Of course; when the husband returned he was in disbelief at the response he got from his wife. She was in tears and very distant until his apologies and compassion reassured her that it was merely a misunderstanding.

Every marriage is different and has its own set of triggers that cannot be compared to any other relationship. What may be okay with one husband may not be okay with yours. What may be okay with one wife may not be okay with yours. I know some spouses that get off of work and they may go to the store, the gym, to a friend's house and never check in with their spouse but for some husbands and wives checking in is a must. Mr. Neale and I are that couple; both of us have triggers that need the reassurance of where we are throughout the day. For him it triggers infidelity, for me it triggers abandonment. If you truly love your spouse you will embrace their triggers and not see them as bondage or control but love and respect for how they feel. It does not matter how silly or ridiculous these triggers may seem to you or your friends, they are very real to the one that is experiencing them. Even when healing has taken place the triggers may still be there. Healing deals with the emotions of the events while triggers deal with the memory of the event. The sting may be gone but the memory often times remain.

CHAPTER 6

DON'T LET YOUR WANT BE GREATER THAN HIS WAIT
(THE PURPOSE OF BEING CONTENT)

*For everything there is a season, a time
for every activity under heaven.*

Sometimes the hardest thing to do in life is wait! Have you ever baked a cake or brownies and when you peek into the oven they look as if they are ready to be consumed but once you get them out of the oven you come to find that they are not fully cooked and undone in the middle? Have you ever ordered a steak and when you received it, it wasn't quite cooked to the perfection that you would have liked? But instead of evaluating the many times you stopped your server inquiring about your meal, you simply get upset and frustrated because it's not to your satisfaction.

Because we have not mastered the art of waiting, we often express our frustrations in life with very distasteful actions. We honk at other vehicles, cursing, yelling and screaming as we sit in a drive through line longer than five minutes. God forbid we end up on the phone with an automated assistant before being transferred to the appropriate department. The buttons on the phone receive severe punishment as we punch harder and harder as if the automated assistant knows or sees our frustration. How about when we meet the dreaded train. Before we can count three box cars go by we have made a u turn and gone 2 miles out of the way, going around, to avoid waiting only to find the train gone once we end up at the same point we would have been had we sat and waited two minutes.

We talk a lot about patience and how much of a virtue it is however; we forget so easily that patience is not only the act of waiting but your attitude while you wait. I know and believe that God has a perfect plan for every one of His creations and only He knows when to release into our lives that one ingredient needed to produce success. Have you ever been rushing and gotten held up by someone in the store and in your mind you are thinking "if it wasn't for blatant disrespect, I would leave her/him standing here alone because I HAVE TO GO!" but then you get down the street and there is a major wreck. What we thought was simply being off schedule was God's hand of protection shielding us from disaster. Have you ever shown up for an event and you hear the words "we only have room for one more" and you were that one? That is what we call perfect timing.

God is never early and certainly never late. Everything God does is perfect, intentional and on time. If your king or queen has not manifested yet, I guarantee you that there is good reason why just trust the process and rest in patience. Just as restlessness and frustration will try to rear its ugly head in all of the examples given, the desire for marriage can mimic some of the same frustrating qualities listed above. In our impatience we rush to partake in things that we desire, such as marriage, without allowing our personal wholeness to get to a place of maturity, perfection and completion.

One of the biggest mistakes you could ever make is rushing into a relationship, marriage, covenant with someone because your ex has someone new. I can't tell you the number of times I have heard someone say "have you seen Joe's new girlfriend?" or "you know she got a new man right?" Who cares! Maybe they completed the waiting process and were ready. Just because you were not ready to remarry at the same time they were doesn't mean something is wrong with you. Do cookies and lasagna take the same amount of time to cook? No! Does a roast take the same amount of cooking time that pizza does? No! Each of these items are beautiful in their own time. After they have endured the recommended heat level and cook time they are a masterpiece within themselves.

In order to accomplish true oneness with your spouse both parties must take full ownership concerning their role in the structure and foundation of their union. If you have found yourself in multiple marriages or relationships you may want to step back and do an examination on yourself. Why am I in and out of relationships? Why is longevity not found in my unions? Is the price too high? Are the roads too rocky? Even if your answer is yes let me warn you, every relationship and every marriage will require work. Every marriage will have some bumpy roads. Yes, every marriage will have a price attached to it!

To abort a relationship solely based on the obstacles that you may face is like saying "I don't want to go to Kansas anymore because it's too many hills, I'll just go to Branson". Baby, let me tell you, it's the same road with the same hills. The question is, are you willing to endure the journey to get to where you want to go. What will help you endure your future journey is remembering what you gleaned from your previous journey. Take note of the detours. Take note of road closures. Take note of the scenery that you didn't care for and make sure that you avoid those obstacles on the next journey.

Let me put this as plainly as I can. I was a medical assistant for 15 years. When working in the hospital setting there were carts called isolation carts that sat outside the room of certain patients. These carts were full of everything needed to protect an individual against what may be awaiting them once they entered that room. Once the individual exits that room they must remove every piece of equipment that was worn previously before they can go to the next room. If they happen to omit the removal process then the person they encounter in the next room is subject to everything the previous person exposed them to. This is true with marriage. If you do not fully strip yourself from everything negative in the marriage or relationship that you have come out of you will simply expose your next spouse to everything that was exposed to you. This stripping process takes time. Are your emotions stable? Are you able to see your flaws and not just the flaws of your ex? Are you able to see your ex and his new love and not be angry? This is a hard one for some, are you able to pray for the wellbeing of your ex? Before entering into a new marriage, remove all of the old pieces connected to the past so that there be no more repeat hurts. No more failed marriages. No more broken homes, only healthy and whole unions, til death do you part.

The Purpose

Content: pleased and satisfied: not needing more.
mentally or emotionally satisfied with things as they are

One of the most important attributes in marriage, as well as singleness, should be contentment! *In whatever state we find ourselves, we should be content.* Couples, never compare your success or process with other couples you may interact with. You know the popular phrase "don't try to keep up with the Jones'"? Well, that is an accurate statement and assessment. Whether it is comparing their public displays of love or their financial status, your marriage is uniquely different from any other and will be built on the components that you possess.

Finances are one of the number one causes of marital conflict. When you find yourself in a financial challenge, don't allow the enemy to drive you apart but rather open up your creative minds. Go on an ice cream date, have a picnic in the park, take a walk together, have a movie night together. You would be surprised at all of the things you can do together that don't cost one cent. These times of hardship should drive you closer together and bring alive your vows to each other for better or worse, richer or poorer. We love to meditate on the lavish trips and vacations we experience together but if truth be told, the aforementioned activities are what really build a solid relationship. These are the times that give way to communication, bonding and one-nesss.

In my first marriage I was a stay at home mother, with 4 small children in the home, while my then husband worked at a local restaurant. We had a plan and a vision and I believe we could have achieved them had we run our race and kept our eyes on our own prize. The problem came when my ex-husband began to want too much too quickly. He would often compare our current situation with that of his siblings. At that time, his brother and his sister in law were both working for the state. Yes, they had small children as well but they had two very good incomes coming into the home. His sister, at that time, was also working for the state and only had two children. I tried repeatedly to show him the contrast of our situations but he would still agree to every event and participate in every outing not taking into account our lack of funds.

Eventually, money (or the lack of it) became our main hurdle and the focus of every argument. Once we divorced, I gathered myself, revisited my original vision, and began to work towards that. Five years after my divorce, I purchased my first home and invited him to come see what had been provided for his children. He was in awe and total disbelief that I had accomplished single what we didn't accomplish married. Despite the fact that I was now a single mother of 4 I ran the race that was given to me and tried, with everything in me, not to compare myself with others but simply master my vision and through patience, I received manifestation.

Although the Lord had blessed me abundantly I still desired to be married again one day. Even in my failed marriage I absolutely loved the state of being a wife but even in my singleness I had to become whole, secure and satisfied in the state that I now found myself in without anything aiding that. Not the aide of someone else. Not the aide of anything else. Simply content with me and me alone. What was hard for me to differentiate between in my singleness was not needing more vs not wanting more! It is perfectly okay and natural for you to desire to be married. It is perfectly fine for you to want companionship but just be sure and very sure that your singleness has run its course. Just as you desire a whole mate, your future mate desires a whole mate. When we move outside of the pre-ordained timing of God we open ourselves up to situations and stresses that could be avoided. Life, singleness, and marriage have their own set of obstacles that must be conquered so why add to that by disregarding the virtue that we quote the most, patience!

Settle! This is a word that has become more common in the single community. Singles everywhere have so affectionately adopted the phrase "but I don't want to settle". Let's address that for a moment. What does it really mean to settle? Does that mean that his income doesn't match yours? Does it mean she still lives at home and is not a homeowner? Does it even mean that he or she doesn't fit your normal type for a mate? ABSOLUTELY NOT!

In my opinion, to settle means that you have moved from a place of patience, moved from an attitude of waiting and you are now willing to accept whatever comes your way to fulfill your own delayed desires. The only problem with this is that you sometimes accept hidden addictions. You sometimes accept dormant spiritual battles. You sometimes accept strongholds, jealousies, generational curses, abuse etc. that most likely will not manifest until those two magical words have been declared which is, I do. When both parties have not successfully passed through the stage of contentment there are unwanted issues that become introduced to the marriage.

Love, not Lust

In the event that one, or both, of the spouses are not whole within themselves prior to marriage, they allow the past insecurities, hurts and memories of past relationships to overflow into their current relationship. Because you are fearful of ending up back in your dark place you guard your present state of love with everything in you and oftentimes to a point of detriment. Your fear causes you to unknowingly suffocate your mate. You begin to hold on tight to what you don't want to lose not realizing that this behavior is turning from genuine love to bondage and eventually lustful desires.

Lust is defined as a strong desire for something or someone. A very powerful feeling of wanting something: strong desire

One may ask, how can you lust for something or someone that belongs to you? Well, the truth of the matter is you can lust for anything in this life. When a person's behavior becomes extreme and excessive it has now gone outside the confines of love and is headed straight towards obsession and lust which ultimately leads to abuse! Love has a security about it within itself. Love accompanies trust. In fact, perfect *love casts out fear*. It would be ideal for the fear you possess concerning your dark place to be driven out during your singleness. Yes, the hurt, rejection and insecurities you face can all be dealt with during a time when no one is affected by the repercussions of your pain. But if not, those fears should most definitely be soothed when you unite with the one that you have declared is your rib or your covering, they should become that missing part.

This is why it is important that the time spent in singleness be spent investing in oneself but instead, we spend the majority of our single lives praying, looking and seeking a mate. The reality is there is just as much joy in singleness as it is in marriage. Likewise; there is just as much depression in marriage as it is in singleness. The key to both is finding contentment; being pleased and satisfied: not needing more in either state.

CHAPTER 7
THE BURDEN

The goal of husband and wife is to, ultimately and foremost, grow together, build together and become one. So often I have witnessed couples that instead of working together on a common goal or task, they appear to compete against one another. How do you compete against yourself? If you win, your wife wins! If you fail, your husband fails! When a mindset of competition is allowed in a marriage neither party is able to value the other's point of view but only how they can somehow "up" the other party. That is not how God intended marriage to be.

I am reminded of a man in the bible that adored his wife and her abilities so much so that thousands of years later, women of all creeds desire to be half of the wife that she was. This man spoke of the value that he saw in his wife. He described and praised her for her ability to use what was in her home to bring in profit. He expressed his gratitude for how she reered his children. He took note of the late nights and early mornings she spent preparing for her family. He called her wife but we call her the Proverbs 31 woman. Because of the care this woman showed to her husband and family, he declares that even he himself is known and recognized by the leaders of that city. This doesn't sound like a marriage of competition but rather one of love and support.

Just for a moment, imagine the most beautiful house you have ever seen built. What if everyone that played a part in the building of that home only emphasized or praised the part that they handled. The mason only praised how sturdy the foundation was because of the skilled work he had contributed. The roofer only praised how well the shingles were laid. What if the glacier felt that his work was the most beneficial because of the precision of his work. As proud as they may feel concerning their contributions to the home it would be foolish to solely focus on their contributions when it took everyone's ability and skill to make a complete home. Many times I have passed by the building of a home and it was draped because it was unfinished and unrefined. This draping was for the purpose of keeping the elements on the outside from destroying what was being built. If your marriage is at a place where it is unfinished and undefined, drape it! That is, keep outsiders out while you continue working on your marriage. When the home comes to a place of perfection (maturity) it is then undraped and all an outsider sees when they pass by is the beauty of the completed work. The goal in marriage is for all outsiders to see the beauty of the completed work, not the chaos in the building of it.

The bible gives a very clear picture of His design for marriage. He reached inside of the man, and essentially made a woman from the rib of that man. The idea is for a woman to become so much one with her husband that she fills the physical void that was left from the removal of that rib. Becoming one does not mean you cease to be a person. The rib was indeed a rib all in itself, it didn't cease to be what it was but moreover it was useful in making something beautiful. Wife, you do not cease to be who you are but you should be instrumental in making something beautiful in the home.

While every strong woman feels that she can do everything that a man can do there are some things that rest solely on the shoulders of a man. Yes woman, you may have occupied the position of an absent father or filled the role of the breadwinner at some point however; part of the weight and distress that you felt was because that was not your burden to bear. It is the man's! God was very clear on the order of the family and His order is that man is the head of the home. With that position comes a burden that many times women take for granted.

Have you ever sat and pondered on all that is required of a man? He has to secure his wife financially. Protect his children from hurt and harm. Cover his home in prayer. Be at every play, recital, football game, cheerleading competition and daddy daughter dance. He is demanded to remember every birthday, anniversary, special holiday and favorite color of his wife in addition to making those things memorable for her year after year. He is expected to paint the house, repair every leak, caulk every hole in the wall, mow the lawn, take the trash out, secure the house before bed, change every flat tire and address the whistling radiator. While some men attain these things, God forbid that he forget even one of the responsibilities listed every now and then, now he is no longer a man in your eyes nor does he care about his household. After 12 years of dedication he is now no good in your sight because of one flaw.

Some may be asking "well, isn't that his job?" Some will dare to say yes, some will say that's a bit much. Whether it is his job or not we can all agree that those are things that we expect and that is undoubtedly quite a load to carry.

Just as women have stepped into men's roles, men too have stepped into women's roles. As out of order as this may seem, it happens. For whatever reason the roles have been reversed, we must not forget that both rolls were created in perfect order. The role of the woman is to be the helpmeet for her husband. Let's take a trip inside the life of that stay at home mother or wife. Do we ever realize what her plate is filled with? She has to address the call of the unsettled children, do the children's hair, wash the laundry, fold the laundry, prepare breakfast lunch and dinner, pay the bills, stretch whatever her husband brings into the home, work with bill collectors, attend parent teacher conferences, help with the children's homework, care for the sick children, care for the sick husband, remember her appointments, remember the appointments of her husband, take the children to their appointments, clean the house, dust the house, vacuum the house, wash the dishes, sew the kids clothes, hem the husbands pants, iron, and be ready every night to please her husband with a smile.

By looking at the list of both roles I don't think either party has room to take the other for granted. The goal is to work together like a fine-tuned machine not to see who can accomplish their duties better.

"Two people are better off than one, for they can help each other succeed. If one person falls, the other can reach out and help. But someone who falls alone is in real trouble. Likewise, two people lying close together can keep each other warm. But how can one be warm alone? A person standing alone can be attacked and defeated, but two can stand back-to-back and conquer. Three are even better, for a triple-braided cord is not easily broken."

Take note at the last statement: three are even better, for a triple-braided cord is not easily broken. Marriage is designed to work independently but when you have God, the third strand, intertwined in your marriage it won't be easily broken. Have you ever heard of a couple divorcing because of something silly? Let's just say he isn't as cleanly as she would like him to be, that is easily broken. What about divorcing because she has gained weight, that is easily broken. Now let's flip it. Have you ever seen a couple stay together after devastation? For example; the loss of a child, not easily broken. Maybe the infidelity of one of the parties, not easily broken.

As stated, marriage is designed to work whether you are a believer or not but when God is the third strand you have more stability. It's like putting a pipe together.

You know that it's on tight, you are sure that it is not cross threaded and feels firm but you still put the pipe tape on to add stability to the pipe. Do believers divorce? Absolutely, but not easily.

CHAPTER 8
OH FOOLISH WOMAN, OH FOOLISH MAN

A true father or mother will always be there for their children in whatever aspect they can be. It is a natural instinct for a father or a mother to want to protect their children from life's hurts regardless of any age limit. We guard them from the kids on the playground and as we watch them play with the kids in the neighborhood. As our children enter adolescence we tend to lend our advice when we feel as if they have a friend or acquaintance that may not mean them any good. In adulthood, we pitch in financially, give advice, watch the grandkids and do whatever is in our power that we feel will help. We desire for our children to be loved with the same love that we love them. This natural instinct to protect does not fade away at any magical age and will surprisingly show up in our children's adulthood as they come to a crossroad of choosing or accepting a spouse.

Oftentimes their choice in a spouse is one that makes us proud and sometimes their choice in a spouse leaves us grieved. Whatever the situation, one thing that must be clear in both emotions is that you cannot pay the cost for your child's ring! What they encounter in their marriage and the price that they must pay is strictly and totally theirs.

MEN:

Fathers, as much as you would love to advise your son on how to handle what might seem like a difficult wife or marital situation, you must be careful to only give advice and not instructions. The word of God tells us, both men and women, to teach the younger generation so yes, by all means teach, train, advise, but you must not instruct. One definition for instruct is *direct or command someone to do something, especially as an official order.* That sounds really harsh huh? Well it is!

It is not your place to instruct your adult son concerning his marriage because he is the one that must pay the cost. So never instruct in a manner such as "let her figure it out on her own" or "let her ask her family". When you instruct in a manner such as this it has the potential to invite division into their home. Have you ever known a couple that had a disagreement and you stepped in to side with the one you thought wanted your support? But when tempers calmed down and things were discussed you became the one both parties were mad with. When you instruct someone to do or not to do something verses advising them you now place yourself in the position to pay the cost (bear the consequences) for their ring, for their relationship. FOOLISH! Only they have to live with the content of their marriage. Them, and them alone are the ones that must count up the cost and the consequences that follow their actions and decisions.

If at any point you are unclear on whether you are overstepping your boundaries with your grown, married children, stop and ask yourself "did I ask her how Jim felt about the situation?" "did I ask him if he had discussed that with Sally?" If your answer is no, then you are occupying a space that their spouse should be occupying. Sure, it's okay to offer advice but never should it take the place of their spouse. It is never okay to weaken the voice of your child's spouse. It is never okay to override the opinion of your child's spouse.

Husbands, under no circumstance do you ever leave your wife uncovered! When you refuse to pay bills that you normally pay, you have left her uncovered. When you withhold sex from her when things are not the way you desire them to be, you have left her uncovered. When you know she is away from your presence and you refuse to answer her phone calls because you are mad at her, you have left her uncovered. FOOLISH! No argument, no disagreement, no deed done should ever cause you to abandon your position as her covering. This does not give women a pass to do whatever it is that she wants to do but do you recall how Adam covered his wife in an earlier chapter? After the God of the universe had pronounced death to them he still spoke life to his wife by calling her mother of the living. Not only did he decree life to his wife but he named her Eve so that every time she is referenced it is a reminder of the correct position of man, the covering of his wife.

WOMEN:

As a mother, you must be conscious not to sabotage your daughter's marriage with phrases like "Baby girl, you deserve better than him" or "You know you can always come home" You are now dealing with a grown woman! A woman that needs guidance with Godly wisdom and not fleshly advice. There becomes a very thin line in reassuring your daughter that you are absolutely there for her if the need arises and misleading her into believing that she can run home every time she is mad at her husband for not washing the dishes like she wanted him too.

Fathers and mothers as much as our children love to declare their independence as adults, our children look to us for advice and guidance in nearly every area of their life to some degree. Our children want to feel that they have made us proud in the decision that they have made however; this is one road that must be traveled without you. After all of the advice and wisdom you have to offer has been offered, the one thing that should never be uttered to your married child is "well, just get a divorce!" FOOLISH!

COUPLES:

Every man needs bonding time with the fellows. The guys that are like minded, that have your best interest at heart and the ones you can confide in concerning struggles in life. However; this does not mean your wife becomes an openly discussed topic. What kind of man would discuss his wife with another man? Her sexual likes and dislikes are absolutely off limits. How she caters to you mentally as well as physically is a restricted area. What she does or does not do around the house is simply not their business. Conversations like this are equivalent to undressing your wife in the presence of your male friends. You are literally striping her by bearing her strengths, flaws, insecurities and weaknesses. Your job and role is to cover and protect her not to strip and harm her. How many times have we heard about marriages being broken apart only for the wife to run off with the husband's best friend? Could the interest in your wife by your friend be the seed that you planted, husband? FOOLISH!

In addition; women, your husbands are not table talk for the next girls gathering. Your husband should not be discussed in detail concerning how he makes love, what his pet peeves are, how he pampers you or how much money he makes. These types of conversations are equivalent to inviting your friend into your bedroom at intimacy time. You do not disclose things about your husband that would entice another woman! You do not open a door that would allow lust, deceit and betrayal to creep in. How many women have lost friends only to find out that the one she felt was closest to her was having an affair with her husband? Could it be that he wasn't the one that enticed her but you were through your subtle conversation? FOOLISH!

Your husband or wife should never be the topic of conversation between you and your friends. Before we get off track let's make one thing clear and very clear, if there is any type of domestic abuse taking place in the home from either spouse most definitely speak up! This is not the time to be silent. When I imply that what goes on between spouses should stay between spouses I am speaking of common and careless conversations within male and female groups that are foolishly allowing destruction to creep into their marriages.

Chapter 9
THE HARD TOPICS

I think this is a good place to talk about some topics that may seem hard to address but must be. In this chapter we will discuss issues that have the potential to be disastrous if left alone.

Step Parents:

Spouses that have previously been married and may have children, do not be naive concerning your children. Watch the interaction between your children and your potential spouse even before vows have been exchanged.

If your children are up in age, pay attention to how your spouse looks at your children. Do you ever notice your spouse looking at your daughter's breast or buttocks? Do you ever notice your spouse looking at your son's crotch, chest or buttocks? Is there excessive hugging or touching their hair? Are you taking note of where your spouse lands their eyes when your children walk into the room? When your children stand to walk out of the room are you observing the body language of your spouse? How does your spouse dress in front of your teenage or young adult children? Sadly, taking note of these actions pertain to both men and women that may be coming into the relationship. Your older children may still be babies in your eyes but they are also young men and women with the potential to be attractive to someone. What you want to prove and verify is pure motherly or fatherly love from your future spouse.

If your children are still young, pay close attention to how your spouse holds your children. Are their hands in the appropriate areas? Do they pat your children on their buttocks? Have you had complaints from your children that they feel uncomfortable around your spouse? In this instance, never brush those complaints off or chalk it up to nothing, listen to your children and never ever turn a deaf ear to the concerns your children are expressing to you.

Infidelity:

In the endeavor to fulfill the covenant that we have entered into we must be fully knowledgeable of the one exception that Moses, under the law, gave for divorce which is adultery! Adultery goes far beyond just a physical act and includes any and all emotional attachments or soul ties to anyone other than your spouse. Now, this doesn't mean that every time your husband laughs at Suzie's joke he is cheating with her or when your wife suggests inviting Joseph to the picnic there's something going on between them. But there is a line that can be crossed and will be evident that things aren't on the up and up, do not ignore the obvious signs.

In this topic we are not only addressing adultery but infidelity as well. Adultery often refers to a physical relationship outside of marriage. It occurs when one partner is sexually involved with another without their partner's consent. Infidelity is the act of being unfaithful to a committed partner.

When "they" make you smile more than your spouse does.... When "they" make you laugh harder than your spouse does.... When you anticipate "their" call more than you do your spouse.... When spending even 15 mins with "them" means more to you than spending time with your spouse, a line has been crossed and I think it's time to evaluate your position with this individual and address it!

Contrary to popular belief, adultery is not as simple as "hello, my name is Scott, would you like to cheat on your husband?" Adultery can be subtle and all of the above listed actions can be seeds that can lead to an inappropriate relationship. These seeds most definitely must not be ignored. Be honest with yourself and your feelings. Evaluate yourself and why your interest may have been piqued for this individual and to such a great degree. Once you have identified that there is an unhealthy desire to be in the presence of this individual it's ok to place some distance between you and them. Even if nothing physical has happened, this is how you prevent it from happening.

Do not ever apologize for the boundaries that you set with the opposite sex if you are married. We are not air heads or macho jerks and understand that every good deed or compliment is not an advancement. However; only you know how something makes you feel. Only you know your comfort level. If you are uncomfortable with the constant compliments on your hair, attire, perfume or cologne express how you feel. If inappropriate touching such as pats on the shoulder, hands laid on your back for long periods or attempts to hug you is the issue, address how you feel. Make your voice heard and if your wishes go ignored do not hesitate to discuss these issues with your spouse. Do not let your guard down in the face of these actions, remember, adultery is subtle. In the event that you do not address these issues and things escalate, questions may arise as to why your concerns were never addressed sooner. This can be misconstrued as deception.

If ever you find yourself in a relationship where infidelity is present please understand that this is not a reflection of you but the sole action and decision of your fragmented mate. There is nothing that one can do to control the actions of another. When someone wants to remain faithful they will.

<u>Sex</u>:

Let's talk about sex. Just as infidelity is not as simple as 1, 2, 3 neither is intimacy and sex with your spouse. We've all heard the phrase *make love to my mind* and it reigns true. Intimacy starts long before the physical act of intercourse. The word of God tells married couples not to deprive one another of sex because it leaves room for the ememy to creep in. Although sex doesn't make a marriage it certainly is a very important component to marriage. When there is not a healthy sex life within a marriage it leaves room for infidelity, soul ties and depression.

First and foremost; sex is the closest physical act of showing your spouse love and why wouldn't you want to express that form of love for your spouse? Sex is the time that you intertwine physically, mentally and emotionally with the one you love. There is no closer way to be physically connected to someone other than the act of sex. This is the perfect time for you to demonstrate your love to your spouse. This is a time where you can release your frustrations, depression or even your joy and happiness. When contemplating marriage it is viatally important to know the sex drive and the sexual needs of your spouse. If your spouse desires to be intimate with you because of their emotional frustration or even just because of their drive it is your obligation as their source to fulfill that desire. If we are endeavoring to follow the order of God then your body, husband, is no longer yours but your wife's. Your body, wife, is no longer yours but your husband's.

When there is not a healthy sex life in a marriage it opens doors for the enemy to present both physical infidelity as well as mental infidelity. Because we have disobeyed the original design of marriage, which is both men and women being virgins when consummation takes place, there are strongholds in our subconscious that have the potential to surface when there is lack of intimacy with our spouse. Remember the phrase we spoke of earlier, *make love to my mind?* When a spouse withholds the most intimate part of the marriage, intimacy in any form is sought. This can be seeking physical intimacy or reminiscing on past encounters of intimacy. This is not a healthy place to be in either instance whether physically or mentally no one should occupy that space except you and your spouse. Counseling, or at the least, communication should be sought to bring clarity to why there is a lack of intimacy in the marriage especially if there was once fire in this area.

I don't want to go on without addressing the lack of sex due to sickness. If you have a spouse that is sick and I'm not talking about a deathly illness but just a simple cold or flu it is not unreasonable to wait until they feel better before you start demanding sex. Although sex is an act in marriage that should be given with love, there should also be a level of sensitivity on behalf of both parties! It is in times like these that love should cover until you are able to consummate again.

Premarital sex:

But if they cannot control themselves, they should marry, for it is better to marry than to burn with passion.

Sex was designed for the confines of marriage. Set your standard and demand that your mate meets you there. But you say that you don't think that they will wait on sex until marriage? The one that genuinely wants you for their spouse will. Have you ever driven by a drive through and the line was around the building and into the street? Have you ever stood at the door of a restaurant twenty minutes before being escorted to your table? What about standing in a line for over an hour to see your favorite performer in concert? The point is, people wait for what they want.

Marriage is a covenant and biblically, a covenant was one that was bonded by blood and unbreakable. When you enter into marriage you enter into a lifelong covenant and the bonding by blood comes when you consummate with your spouse. The seamen that a husband releases intermingles with the broken blood vessels inside the vaginal walls of his wife. Covenant has just taken place. To partake in the act of sex before marriage only invites soul ties and strongholds that sometimes take years for someone to get free from.

Have you ever heard someone say that they are in love with two people? Honestly, they are not truly in love with both, if either. What may be the case is that they possibly are in love with one and tied to the other one.

The need to be loved sexually is a natural desire and there is a solution for those that feel as if they need the physical interaction with the opposite sex. Get married! Of course, one should not simply get married because of the lack of self-control but what this statement suggests is to be realistic concerning your needs within your relationship.

For the most part, we know that the wedding, the venue, the flowers and all of the glitz and glamor of the wedding is for the woman. However; if your future husband is expressing to you that his needs are growing more intense, why continue to wait another six months only to put on a show for people that won't even remember the details of the show that you are so proud to display.

I have been on both sides of this topic. Marriage one, we gave in to our fleshly desires and entered the act of premarital sex resulting in the birth of our son and a quick ending.

Marriage two, we agreed that we would wait until marriage before partaking in the act of sex that would ultimately make us one. We dated for eleven months while planning our wedding. During our planning time we revisited our wedding date several times to see if it was still feasible to stick to the original date as desires began to intensify. We held on to the agreement that we made and made it to our wedding day. On the night of our honeymoon he was able to present himself to me and I was able to present myself to him undefiled. The two experiences are uncomparable. Wisdom says, it's better to marry than to burn in your flesh so if your mate desires all of you and not just a piece of you they will wait or they will marry.

Finances:

This is a topic that must be discussed in detail prior to marriage. Who budgets better? Who brings in the income if not both? Whose bank account will be used? Will there be separate accounts? How will the bills be paid? Will the bills be split? These are all very valid issues that have the potential to become a distraction in marriage.

9 times out of 10 when a couple marries there are already bank accounts, houses and business in general that have been established by both parties and that is understandable and expected. Now a merge has to take place but the question is what is best for you?

This is not a subject that is one size fits all. There is no right or wrong answer to how to handle finances within a marriage but simply a very clear agreement between both spouses on what works best for your marriage. What may work for one couple may not work for the next. In any event; what must not ever take place under the umbrella of finances is manipulation. If you are the breadwinner and there is a need in the home, the need must be met. If there has already been an agreement set in place concerning how finances will be handled, it must not and cannot be changed based on the fluctuating feelings of either spouse.

Prenuptial agreements:

Tell me you want to argue before marriage without telling me you want to argue before marriage. This topic can mean so many different things across a wide variety of situations. Some may view it as a proving point that you are really marrying them solely for them with no ulterior motives. Some may view it as a red flag, feeling that there is already a permanent wall separating them and their spouse.

For some prenups are the way to go and for others it is an absolute no go. Even in the event that both parties agree to a prenup it needs to be evaluated thoroughly to see if it is the best situation for your marriage. What is the reason that you feel a prenup is needed? Are you guarded? Do you have trust issues? Do you see your relationship as short term?

If these questions are not dealt with before you enter into marriage you will confront them sooner rather than later. How can two become one if there is division before the commitment? How will you honor for richer or for poorer when you have already secured your riches? How can your wife fully submit when she feels she is left to provide for herself? How can your husband cover you properly when he feels you are sufficient outside of him?

Cell Phones:

Should you lock your phone? Should your spouse have the code to your phone? Should your spouse be allowed to go through your phone? Those are all questions that must be addressed within each individual marriage. There is not just one correct answer for these questions as each marriage is different.

It's my belief that every cell phone in America should have a privacy code or lock on it for the purpose of loss or theft. I am aware and accept that everyone does not believe the way that I believe as my husband never has a code on his phone. Never does he lock his phone. And lastly, never does he even have the volume turned up for phone calls. Whatever your belief is concerning cell phones it is a known fact that cell phones can be a major issue in marriage.

Marriages have literally been torn apart behind cell phones. Whatever trust level you and your spouse have established should be clear and drama free when this subject arises however; don't be naive, this trust level can be destroyed with one hidden text message or one phone call from that "friend" of the opposite sex.

What is communicated on your cell phone is just as critical and damning as what you communicate to someone face to face. There should be no reason for a spouse to feel intimidated by what they feel may be taking place right under their nose through their spouse's cell phone. Some would say that they can't help if their spouse is paranoid, it's their problem but I beg to disagree. It is your responsibility to make your spouse know that they are the most important person in your life. If you can't ever answer your phone in front of them that may be a problem. If you are up texting late at night or in the wee hours of the morning, that may be a problem. If you have to go to the bathroom, walk away from your spouse or turn in a different direction from your spouse before you can answer a text or decline a call...... this most certainly may be a problem. Just with any other issue in marriage, this topic must be addressed if any of the actions above are noted. If everything is as innocent as your spouse says it is, this issue should resolve peacefully.

Social Media:

Where do we begin with the world of social media? It has become the new era of communication. We use it to connect to long time friends. We use it to conduct and promote business. For the most part we use it for entertainment. This harmless act of communication has become a platform for arguments and misunderstandings in marriages world wide. Just as anything has the ability to be abused, social media falls into that category.

If I like her picture will my wife think something is arye? If I comment on his post will my husband suspect something is more than a simple comment? Facebook, Twitter, Instagram, Whatsapp are all tools that are quite useful when used in the capacity in which they were created. For example; I had a very close friend that lived in South Carolina that passed away. Her niece found me on Facebook, messaged me through messenger and informed me. Because this tool was used in the way that it was designed I was able to receive this news and travel to pay my respects.

The problem with social media only arises when it is abused. Recall the hidden messages and locked phones we discussed above? When compliments can no longer be posted on your page but now need to be sent privately you may need to address that early. Now, we understand that everyone that offers a compliment does not have ulterior motives but let's say that the person that sent the private message saw you out in public. Would they need to take you to a remote private place before they could compliment you? Or would they simply say in front of everyone "you look really nice today". Just as no one needs to send you a private message, you should have no reason to send anyone else a private message. The bottom line is respect! If you would not feel comfortable with this kind of behavior from your spouse then have enough respect not to put your spouse in this position.

Domestic Abuse:

God forbid that either spouse experiences domestic abuse within a marriage but we will briefly touch on this issue as we know that unfortunately it is relevant in the world that we live in.

This may be one of the hardest topics to address because first and foremost, the vow we make to both God and man is to be devoted and loyal to our spouse till death.

The word of God only gives two causes that can release someone from the covenant of marriage. The act of adultery and the state of abandonment. Even though you are allowed to resolve your marriage based on these acts you are still not commanded too. Although the thought of forgiving someone for the act of abuse, of any kind, is hard to grasp for some, it is possible. Anything and everything is forgivable if you allow yourself to forgive. No one stays the same, we are ever changing entities with the capabilities of reform. As with any other issue in marriage, pride is the one agent that will hinder forgiveness.

The act of forgiveness is a two party activity. The one forgiving has to have the fortitude to move past the act of the event and the one needing forgiveness has to show change. Change is an act of becoming new. Your mate must be able to behold the process of the new you.

If you find yourself in a place of abuse and your spouse is not actively seeking professional help, through counseling and or with medication, you need to get before the Lord and get a personal word for your situation.

It is better not to make a vow than to make a vow and break it! While we reject the gift of singleness and rush into commitments that we are not ready for, we easily forget the vows that we have made before God and man.

I am not suggesting that God's desire is for you to be a victim of abuse and I sincerely pray that you never find yourself in that situation but in the same breath I could never instruct you to do something that goes against the vow that you have made to your God and spouse. In the event that your decision is to divorce and part ways, it would have to be 100% a personal judgement call.

No one has the authority to instruct or encourage anyone to divorce. God's instructions to those that have committed themselves with a vow is to *let no man put asunder.*

CHAPTER 10
THE DARK PLACES

This chapter is one that is dear to my heart because I feel that I lived here for a large portion of my life. As much as we hate to address it and whether we admit it or not, every person has a dark place.

A dark place is a place and time in your life that you never want to visit again, a place you fear even when you simply think of it. If you struggled to come out of poverty and are now living a comfortable life, poverty is indeed your dark place. If you suffered through infidelity but now live in a secure marriage, then infidelity is your dark place. If you have experienced a divorce and find yourself in marriage #2 then there is no doubt that divorce is your dark place and every shadow of a dispute and every sign of an argument will bring up the memory of your dark place. Whether it is the loss of a child, being molested, overcoming addiction, overcoming poverty, losing a job or your house burning down there is a place we all fight to never see again.

Because our fear of these dark places are so overwhelming, we sometimes cannot enjoy our current state of being because we are secretly fighting within ourselves to never end up "there" again. We become workaholics because inwardly we are fighting to never struggle again. We live insecure in our current marriage because we are always on guard for possible infidelity. We shelter ourselves and forfeit healthy relationships because of past abuse and experiences. That is no way to live for you or your spouse. What you go through, your spouse goes through. It would be ideal for these issues and insecurities to be resolved before marriage but in the event that they aren't you must find time and space to become healed emotionally from these issues. The best asset you could bring to the table of marriage would be self- sufficiency in your emotions, thoughts and spirit. Hmm, you thought I was going to say finances huh? That will come, especially if you two can build together but until both mates are emotionally stable, your house will remain in shambles. What good is money if you are miserable?

Shadows

Shadows: *A reflected image*

Sadly, every dark place is associated with shadows. These are images that are not real and are no longer present in your life but seek to haunt you long after you have escaped the horror of your dark place. Remember, David did not inquire of God concerning death itself but he sought the Lord concerning the valley of the "shadow" of death and declared that he would not fear. Oftentimes, these shadows are just as painful as the actual event if not dealt with.

In marriage, it is imperative that you be fully delivered, healed and whole when dealing with your mate or these shadows will shatter your marriage. What and how someone feels or perceives a situation is sometimes the only reality they can relate to. Until these shadows are eradicated from your life, no matter the amount of love and affirmation you receive will ever suffice. When you lack trust, you will always be paranoid, always feel rejected and unwanted and ultimately unloved. There is only a certain level of love that your mate can give that will fill your void, you must be an active participant in the love process, not only for your mate but for yourself as well. When you allow the shadows of life to infiltrate your trust level, misery is inevitable!

The absence of trust is torment

Torment for you because your mind is not at peace but is constantly thinking about where he/she may be. What he/she might be doing and who he/she might be doing it with. You are terrified that someone else has the power and influence to maintain the attention of your mate.

Torment for your mate because they feel that all of their efforts to secure you in your relationship have been in vain. No matter how many times he/she tells you that they will never leave you, there is still doubt. No matter how many times they tell you they love you, there is still questioning. They feel that nothing they do or say can fill that space where trust should reside.

Perfect Love

Perfect love casts out fear therefore; when you allow the relationship between you and your spouse to fully mature you will come to see that a lot of the fears you once had have now begun to dissipate. It is now that you can begin to live the life of marriage that God designed and one He desires for you to live.

CHAPTER 11
DON'T REJECT
THE REACH

*N*o history of marriage has ever had a success story that didn't include a disagreement or argument at some point in time. The very first couple that we relate to is Adam and Eve and even they clearly did not agree on everything. What's important to master in marriage is forgiveness. My husband and I often enjoy looking back over the words of encouragement that were given to us at the time of my bridal shower and our wedding. What was most consistent was don't go to bed mad at each other and always say I love you when you leave each other.

Of course, after a disagreement there is a cool down period which is vital and necessary for both parties however; when the argument is over let it be over. When you feel that touch on your back you must not pull away! The invitation to a movie must not be ignored! This is your spouse reaching for you, somewhat testing the waters or checking the atmosphere for reconciliation and if they still feel resistance the words "I'm sorry" may still be a ways away.

Apologies do not always come in the form of verbal expression. Yes, it is important to address topics that cause disturbance in the marriage but it has its place. Allow both parties to calm down and give the situation time to settle then deal with it but until that time comes, don't reject whatever reach your spouse may extend. When he comes and sits beside you on the couch, stay. When she makes your lunch for the next work day, take it. That's their reach!

Pride will cause a simple misunderstanding to halt forward motion and progress in your marriage. The inability to accept the reach that is extended to you allows a wedge to grow between the two of you which is ultimately dividing the union. The word admonishes the husband to honor his wife as the weaker vessel so husband's, you may be the one that has to give in per se but as long as you continue to be divided, your prayers are hindered.

CHAPTER 12
THE TWO SHALL BECOME ONE FLESH

*N*ot all marriages live in a state of crisis. Not all marriages are regretted. Believe it or not there are some marriages that actually function the way they were designed too. Nevertheless; even on your best day of marriage, your marriage could use a tune up. Who would ever wait until their car ran completely out of gas before they added gas to it? Who would ever wait until they had absolutely no food in their home before getting more? We give attention to these things beforehand to prevent problems before they arise. In marriage it is wise to connect with a marriage group or attend counseling sessions before things are what we would call on the rocks. Routine maintenance on anything that you place value on only shows that you take pride in it and you want it to last.

As with any relationship in life we must strive to live in harmony with those around us whether it be our siblings, in-laws, co-workers and even our spouse. Have you ever worked on a job site and there was so much tension between the workers that it was unbearable? Have you ever walked into an establishment and you could tell by the way the workers talked to each other and the way they interacted with each other that they really didn't care to be sharing the same space with them? Often it's because someone is not in sync with the flow of that company.

As much as we would like to believe that our game face is finely tuned, outsiders are able to detect when someone is not in sync with the flow of their marriage. Body language, gestures and tone of voice will tell it all. Because we have abused the phrase "what happens in this house stays in this house" we don't know when to properly use it. Well, your marriage is one of those times! No one should be able to gauge the temperature of your marriage simply by your attitude. Learn to forgive quickly and often. When there is not a mutual understanding of the roles within your marriage your prayers become hindered hence further frustration and separation.

As stated; I worked in the medical field for 15+ years as a Medical Assistant and worked with many doctors from clinical settings to hospital settings. One of the qualities that I found most consistent in both settings was the ability to know the doctor that you worked with or to become one with him in a sense. If I happened to work in an area that I normally didn't I would sometimes watch my co-workers and how they did things with their doctor and I would sometimes ask "why didn't you do........." or I would say "hmm, I would have…." Their response would be "he doesn't like it done that way" mind you many times these were doctors in the same clinic or hospital. Because I hadn't spent enough time with that particular doctor I felt on edge and self-conscious as to whether he was pleased with my performance even though I knew my job inside and out. Now, when I worked in my area, with my doctor I was in my zone. I knew what he wanted and how he wanted it done. Depending on the reason for my patient's visit, I could have a minor test run, results back and everything set up before the doctor hit the room. This allowed the doctor to diagnose and treat without triaging the patient again (which was my job) causing frustration from him as well as the patient, not to mention it cut down on patient wait time. To him I was thorough and efficient in my interactions with him and what he wanted. While working in other areas that I wasn't quite familiar with, those doctors would pull me aside and say "you are doing a great job but let me see the patient first". Was I offended? ABSOLUTELY not! I was aware that I didn't know that doctor on the level that I knew mine but the more time I spent with him the more I was able to provide him with the quality of work that he wanted, needed and ultimately was pleased with.

Marriage is no different! If we don't spend enough time with our spouse we will never be able to provide them with the quality of marriage that they want, need and ultimately pleases them. We would love to believe that marriage is stress free and a flawless state of being when in reality marriage has its natural ups and downs. It has been said that it takes five years or more to BEGIN to truly know your mate. I don't mean what their favorite color is, what their favorite drink is, where they hang out or who their friends are. All of those superficial things can be learned about your co-workers and acquaintances! When I say to know your mate, I mean being so in tune with them that you are able to fully and accurately make up the deficit in their life. I am talking about knowing your mate literally as well as you know yourself. When your mate is irritable or their behavior changes from the norm, is it because they haven't eaten? Is it because they are sleep deprived? Are you able to lay your hand on your mate and feel the calm come over them? Are you able to quietly say "babe, come lay down and rest, you're tired"? Being this in tune with your spouse can defuse a number of arguments because you will not be reacting to the issue at hand but will be able to see and understand the underlying cause of the issue and resolve it sometimes without them even being aware of what just happened.

However; in order to become one with your mate the way God wants you to become one, you have to actually let down your guards and walls and become vulnerable in ways that may be very uncomfortable for you. In becoming one, you must be clear on some facts. Is your mate spontaneous? Is your mate a planner? Does your mate like to be in the public or does your mate like to sit at home? Is your mate a giver or is your mate conservative? I could go on but I think you get the point. These are questions that need to be addressed prior to saying "I do" because they have the potential to cause major problems if not talked out.

I'm not quite sure where the misconception came from that you instantly become one when you say I do but becoming one is a process, some longer than others but nevertheless; it is a process. Even if you marry young and you have had years of being under the rule of your parents and answering to them, it is not the same as answering to a spouse. Answering to someone else, being submissive to someone (men and women), and being concerned with someone else's needs takes time to master.

Sexual frustration, which oftentimes are the cause of infidelity, is one of the leading causes of divorce. When you have sex with someone there is a bond, or tie if you will, that takes place. Have you ever wondered why you lose your sex drive for your spouse? Before marriage, some felt as if they couldn't live life without sex. Many desired to get married on the basis of fulfilling the Holy Scripture which states not to "burn in your flesh" so what happened? Now that your marriage bed is Holy in the sight of God and man, have you ever stopped to ask yourself why there is not much going on under the sheets? Well, I will tell you why. The enemy does not want marriages to establish the bond (or tie) that takes place during physical and sexual intimacy. It is a spiritual attack that causes either mate to lack the desire to satisfy their spouse sexually. We tend to phrase it like this, "I'm not attracted to him/her anymore". Sure, a marriage does not solely consist of sex but the word of God is clear in that the woman's body is no longer hers but her husbands. Likewise; the husband's body is no longer his but his wife's. Many women reject this point of view because of the lack of understanding behind it.

This does not mean that you have lost your identity and are now the possession of someone. What it means is that your body, wife, is now the place where he comes to be fulfilled. Your body, husband, is now the place where she comes to be fulfilled. You no longer are concerned with only fulfilling your selfish desires but now you fulfill the desires of your spouse.

As married couples we should seek and desire the satisfaction of our spouse. It is of the highest importance to understand the role of sex in marriage and that men and women experience different emotional rewards from the act. Most women, when they are stressed, have a decline in the desire for sex where most men, when they are stressed, have a heightened desire for sex. You as a spouse, men and women, must know and recognize when a release is needed. Your spouse should be able to come home and release to you everything that their day consisted of whether it be stress, happiness, joy, defeat, failure or just simple pleasure.

Blissfulness not Bondage

As the head of the home, men, you must endeavor to assert authority without making your wife feel like she is in bondage! Where were you at 5:30? Who did you go with? How long were you there? What did you buy? If your wife is truly submitted to you then that type of information will be disclosed to you without the iron fist from you. You must not allow your insecurities of past relationships to cause bondage in your present relationship. The word of God speaks of husbands dealing with the wife according to knowledge therefore; you need to use wisdom in every area of your marriage. Remember, just as you may be very inquisitive because of past hurts, she may be very reserved because of past hurts and vice versa.

The idea is to become one by resisting those things that will only cause further division. Am I saying you can't inquire on the specifics of your spouse? Contrary; but as we have mentioned repeatedly, tone is the key that will turn the door to chaotic resistance or peaceful submission.

CONCLUSION

The words contained and summarized in this writing is not the summation of what marriage is but simply a beginning to understand what price must be paid as a result of your I do and the ring that you proudly display.

In a world so crazy I am not oblivious to believe that divorce does not take place. Nevertheless; that does not excuse us from the responsibilities given to us by God through our wedding vows which is to love, honor, cherish, obey until death do us part. My desire and heartfelt goal is to broaden your mindset concerning what marriage entails and the real cost both men and women pay for their ring. Just as marriage is not solely made up of picket fences, landscaped lawns, vacations and bliss neither does it solely consist of fights, arguments, slander and depression. Marriage is beautiful when executed the way it was designed.

My sincere prayer is that you allow yourself the pleasure and the joy of becoming one with your spouse. Leadership and submission are not words of taboo but rather words of power. The strength of leadership and the peace of submission are beautiful when exerted properly.

The Cost of The Ring I will gladly pay

Lord, we thank you for the sanctity of marriage and all that it encompasses. We believe that you are able to restore what may seem damaged beyond repair. We make a conscious effort to be more attentive to our spouse in order to close every area of separation that may exist in our marriage

Because marriage is a direct reflection of Christ and His bride we ask that you make us one with our spouse as Christ has become one with His bride. We will be as steadfast in patience with our spouse just as You are as steadfast with Your bride.

Husbands

As the head of my home I will cover and protect my bride as passionately as You cover Your bride. I will never leave nor forsake my wife just as you have promised to never leave nor forsake Your bride.

I will provide for my wife with the same consistency that You provide for Your bride.

Wife

As a submitted wife to my husband I will imitate the submission of Your bride. I will honor, love and obey the leadership of my husband just as Your bride honors You.

I will be quick to repent to my husband just as Your bride repents to You.

Husband and Wife

We renounce and shut out the voice of every serpent that would attempt to come into our marriage to deceive and divide.

We thank You that as our marriage mirrors Christ and His bride and it is equally as beautiful and whole.

Thank you Lord for supplying us with a flawless plan and perfect example of success for our marriage through Christ and His bride.

Mr & Mrs. Neale

ABOUT THE AUTHOR

Twyla Harrison-Neale is a repeat author with her first literary work "Thou Shalt be Saved" releasing in 2005. She is a college graduate, licensed minister and proud mother of 5 children and 1 bonus child. She has experienced the life of marriage, divorce, single motherhood and remarriage. As she conquered every stage that was presented to her she came to understand the true meaning of family. She married young and divorced early only to walk a life of singleness for the next nineteen years. She has experienced some of the same lows in marriage that others have but desires to help many experience the true highs of marriage that she has now found. She sees the extensive burden that both husbands and wives carry and will show readers how this burden can be eased by becoming one with one another and sharing the load. She understands the hard work and sacrifices that must be made within a marriage and offers tools that can result in successful outcomes. Her heart and passion is to help marriages that may have found themselves in the low phase of their marriage to realize that it really is only a phase, keep fighting until you see the reward of your labor.

Printed in the United States
by Baker & Taylor Publisher Services